SPACE PUZZLES:

Curious Questions and Answers

About the Solar System

Also by Martin Gardner

NEVER MAKE FUN OF A TURTLE, MY SON

PERPLEXING PUZZLES AND TANTALIZING TEASERS

SPACE PUZZLES:

Curious Questions and Answers About the Solar System

by Martin Gardner

Illustrated with diagrams and photographs
Drawings by Ted Schroeder

SIMON AND SCHUSTER   NEW YORK

For

Jeg and Tog

Thanks are due to the following for permission to use the indicated photographs:

All Around the Moon by Jules Verne, Dover Publications, Inc., New York: p. 65

American Museum of Natural History: pp. 9 (art work by Planetarium Staff, Hayden Planetarium), 22, 24, 26, 27 (top left), 82

Lowell Observatory: pp. 41, 44, 86

Meteor Crater Enterprises, Inc.: p. 20

NASA: pp. 13, 29, 31, 66, 83

New Mexico State University Observatory: p. 84

Jules Bucher, *Photo Researchers, Inc.*: p. 27 (top right)

Yerkes Observatory, University of Chicago, Williams Bay, Wis.: pp. 27 (bottom), 33, 40, 48, 50, 53, 54, 55

Diagrams by Libra Studios: pp. 12, 29, 35, 36, 57, 61, 75, 76, 78, 80, 88, 89, 90, 94

Text Copyright © 1971 by Martin Gardner
Illustrations Copyright © 1971 by Ted Schroeder
Published by Simon and Schuster, Children's Book Division
Rockefeller Center, 630 Fifth Avenue
New York, New York 10020
First Printing
SBN 671–65182–X Trade
SBN 671–65183–8 Library
Library of Congress Catalog Card Number: 78–144777
Manufactured in the United States of America

Contents

Introduction

Experiments have been made in which hungry chimpanzees were allowed to choose between eating and looking through a suddenly uncovered opening to see into a room in which electric trains and other devices were operating. The chimps actually preferred to watch rather than eat. This ancient, monkeylike curiosity, a desire to know what is happening, is the main reason why most scientists do what they do.

It is true, of course, that scientists have other motives. Like everybody else they want to be paid for their work. They enjoy fame. They know also that their discoveries can often reduce human misery or make life happier. They can find ways to prevent polio, to design color television sets, to bring fresh water to barren deserts. For most scientists, however—certainly for the greatest ones—the basic motive is a desire to *know*. Just as mountain climbers say they have to climb a high mountain "because it is there," so astronomers want to solve the mystery of, say, Jupiter's Great Red Spot simply because it, too, "is there." The Red Spot which they see with their telescopes is like the electric train the monkeys see through the opening in a wall. Like the monkeys, the astronomers are consumed with curiosity.

All sciences have a beauty in the precise structure and simplicity of their laws, but some are more beautiful than others. Surely astronomy is one of the most beautiful. It has a sweep and grandeur that arouses awe in all but the dullest minds. This collection of puzzling astronomical questions is intended to stimulate your sense of wonder about an inconceivably tiny portion of the universe, the solar system. This is the name astronomers use for our sun, its nine known planets, and all the other bodies (such as moons, asteroids and comets) that are held captive by the sun's strong gravity. Our sun, as perhaps you already know, is in a gigantic two-armed spiral galaxy called the Milky Way which contains billions of other suns. Millions of those suns may have planets circling around them that are very much like the planets that go around our own sun. Millions of those planets may teem with some kind of life. Life on these alien worlds may be similar to life on earth, or it may be entirely different in ways we cannot now even imagine. Our galaxy in turn is only one of billions of other galaxies. Perhaps in a second book we can take up some puzzling questions about this vast universe that lies far beyond the orbit of Pluto, our outermost planet.

Meanwhile here are some puzzling problems about our own solar system. Now that humanity has made its first tottering steps into space, now that our astronauts will soon be leaving bootprints on Mars and other

The Milky Way Galaxy

planets, astronomy is certain more and more to dominate the news. We are on the threshold of hundreds of fresh, startling, unexpected new discoveries about the solar system. No person can call himself educated who does not know at least the basic facts about that stupendous, fantastic clockwork of giant spheres, not made by us, on one of which we are (or should be) astonished to find ourselves riding.

MARTIN GARDNER

Chapter 1 | THE EARTH

Our earth, the third planet from the sun, is the "space-ship" on which all humanity is traveling. As it moves in its yearly orbit around the sun, it whirls like an enormous top, making one complete turn every 23 hours, 56 minutes and 4 seconds. This rotation makes the sun, moon and stars appear to rise in the east and move slowly across the sky until they set in the west. The earth's axis—an imaginary straight line around which it spins— is tilted about 23 degrees from being perpendicular to the plane of the earth's orbit or path around the sun. This tilt alters the amount of sunlight that falls on various parts of the earth at various times. It is this variation in sunlight that, in some latitudes, causes the four seasons: winter, spring, summer and fall. South of the equator the seasons are the opposite of ours. When it is winter in the United States it is summer in Argentina and Australia.

The earthship cruises around the sun in a slightly

11

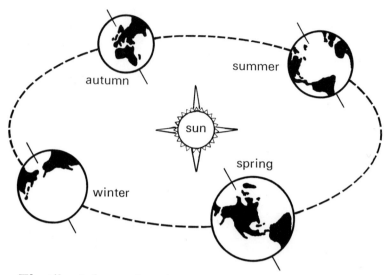

The tilt of the earth as it revolves around the sun alters the amount of sunlight being received in different latitudes. This variation in sunlight causes the four seasons, which are shown here for the Northern Hemisphere.

elliptical orbit at 18½ miles per second. It takes about 365¼ days for the earth to complete one trip around the sun. That extra quarter of a day explains why, every four years, we have to add a 366th day to our year to make "leap year." If we did not do this, the seasons would keep arriving later and later in the calendar every year.

In addition to its two basic motions, rotating on its axis and revolving around the sun, the earth is also carried through space as the sun moves through our galaxy of stars at about 12 miles per second. The galaxy itself is rotating, too. Finally, our galaxy belongs to a cluster of galaxies which also is moving through the universe. There are, therefore, at least five different kinds of motion that our earthship has. We can't "feel" any of them, just as someone in a smoothly flying airplane is unable to sense the plane's motion. If you toss a penny in the air on a plane, the air and penny move with the plane. The coin goes up and down exactly as it would if the plane were at rest on the ground. Since the earth carries its air along with it as it moves, there is no "wind" to let us know which way it is moving.

Although millions of people in the past believed the earth to be flat, many ancient Greeks were convinced it was a ball. Aristotle, the great Greek philosopher and scientist, argued (correctly) that the earth is spherical, since, during an eclipse of the moon, the earth's shadow

Full view of the earth from ¼ million miles away, taken by Apollo 10 Astronauts. The west coast of North America can be seen just right of center; the remainder of the land mass is obscured by cloud cover.

on the moon has a circular edge. Eratosthenes, a third-century Greek astronomer, actually computed the earth's diameter so accurately that he missed the right figure by only about 70 miles!

Centrifugal force is an outwardly directed force that arises when there is circular movement. If you spin a wet top, for example, centrifugal force causes drops of water to fly outward from the top's surface. Because the earth spins as fast as it does, centrifugal force made it bulge slightly at its equator at a time in the distant past when it was less rigid than it is today. The earth has retained that bulge ever since. At the equator the earth's diameter is a little more than 7,986 miles but from pole to pole it is closer to 7,900 miles. This flattening at the poles gives the earth a shape that is called an "oblate spheroid." In recent years more precise measurements by artificial satellites have shown that in addition to this oblateness the earth is also slightly pear-shaped, its smaller end being at the north. Surprisingly, Christopher Columbus once expressed his belief that the earth was shaped like a pear. It was no more than a guess, but it has turned out to be a good one!

How was the earth first formed? The question obviously is part of the more general question of how the entire solar system evolved. Many different theories have been advanced and there is still much disagreement among astronomers over which theory is best. The most widely accepted view at present is that there originally was a vast spinning cloud of dust and gas. Gravity caused the cloud to form a dense inner core which became the sun. While this was happening, huge whirlpools formed here and there in the cloud. Over millions of years the whirlpools condensed into solid spheres which became the planets, while smaller whirlpools around the planets condensed to become moons. The spinning of the primordial cloud would explain why all the planets and most of their moons travel along their orbits in the same direction.

The earth's atmosphere was quite different in past geologic ages before life made its first appearance on the planet. Now almost four-fifths of the atmosphere is nitrogen. Oxygen makes up about one-fifth, and about one percent is a mixture of carbon dioxide, water vapor, argon and other gases.

Puzzling Question 1:

About three-fourths of the earth is covered with water. Imagine the earth reduced to the size of a billiard ball and dried with a towel. You run your fingertips over the surface. Would you be able to feel its mountains and ocean floors?

Puzzling Question 2:

If you climb to the top of a high mountain, you will weigh a tiny bit less than you did before, because the earth's gravitational pull decreases as you go farther from its surface.

What happens to your weight when you go down to the bottom of a deep mine? Is it the same as on the surface, or is it more or less?

Puzzling Question 3:

A scale has a platform large enough for a horse to stand on. If a man and horse are weighed separately and their weights are added, the sum will be a trifle more than if the man climbs on the horse and the two are weighed together. Can you explain why?

Puzzling Question 4:

Many science fiction stories and novels have been written about tunnels that go straight through the center of the earth and come out the other side. If such a

16

tube went from the north pole to the south pole, and you fell into one of its open ends, exactly what would happen to you? You may remember that Alice wondered about this question while she was falling down the rabbit hole into Wonderland.

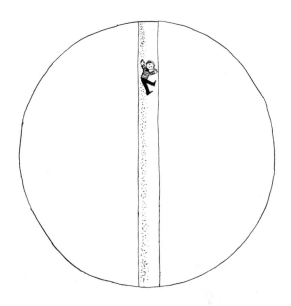

Puzzling Question 5:

Charles L. Dodgson, a British mathematician who wrote the two *Alice* books under the pen name of Lewis Carroll, also wrote a long fantasy novel called *Sylvie and Bruno*. In the second half of this work, a whimsical "German Professor" explains how a "gravity train" operates:

"Each railway is in a long tunnel, perfectly straight: so of course the *middle* of it is nearer the center of the globe than the two ends: so every train runs halfway *down*-hill, and that gives it force enough to run the *other* half *up*-hill."

Would such a gravity train actually work?

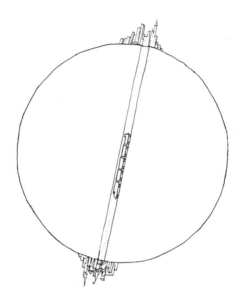

Puzzling Question 6:

It is often said that a person standing at the bottom of a deep well could look up during the daytime and see the stars. Is this true?

Puzzling Question 7:

A certain table weighs ten pounds. If you put this table in outer space, then placed the earth on top of it, how much would the earth weigh on the table?

|METEORS

A meteor is a piece of rock or metal moving through space. When it enters the earth's atmosphere, at a speed faster than that of a rifle bullet, friction causes it to get white-hot and vaporize, leaving behind a glowing trail of gas and dust. We call this a "shooting star." Most shooting stars are produced by pellets about the size of a pea. If the meteor is much larger, it may not burn up completely and part of it will land on earth. The rock that survives is called a meteorite.

The United States has a large crater near Winslow, Arizona, that was produced some fifty thousand or more years ago by the impact of a giant meteorite. In June 1908 a large meteorite fell—perhaps the sudden heat of friction caused it to explode in the air—in Siberia, destroying a huge section of a forest. In 1954 a nine-pound meteorite crashed through the roof of a house in Sylacauga, Alabama, and struck a housewife on her hip while she was napping on a sofa. Fortunately she was not

Northern Arizona's Great Meteor Crater, also known as the Barringer Crater, near Winslow, Arizona.

seriously injured. It was the first authenticated case of a person actually being hit by a falling star.

If one is patient enough he can see a shooting star or two on any clear night, but when the earth passes through a swarm of meteors, hundreds or even thousands of shooting stars can be counted in a single hour. This event is called a "meteoric shower." The largest swarm of meteors (periodically encountered by the earth) travels an elliptical path around the sun that extends out past the orbit of Uranus. The meteors are strewn along their orbit for such an enormous distance that every November the earth is sure to pass through a part of the swarm. Usually the earth "catches" a sparse portion, but about every 33 years it catches the densest part of the swarm and then the sky puts on a marvelous display of fireworks. The most brilliant such displays were in 1866 and 1867, but there was a good one in 1966 and another can be expected about 1999. The meteors in this swarm are called the Leonids because when they enter the earth's atmosphere they seem to come from a spot in the constellation of Leo the lion.

Puzzling Question 8:
During a Leonid shower the meteors' fiery trails are always much more numerous in the early morning hours from midnight to sunrise than in late evening

hours from sunset to midnight. Can you think of the reason?

The Leonid meteor shower of November 14, 1867, as seen near Sandy Hook, New Jersey.

Chapter 2 | THE SUN

The sun is the star around which our earth and its eight sister planets revolve. Compared with the billions of other stars in our galaxy it is just a medium-size star, but compared with the earth it is a gigantic ball of glowing gas with a diameter of 864,000 miles, a little more than 100 times the earth's diameter. If we imagine the earth the size of a BB shot, the sun would be about the size of a basketball. Its distance from us is close to 93 million miles.

Without the enormous energy and heat that we get from the sun, our earth would be a freezing, lifeless planet. Only in recent decades have scientists understood where the sun's energy comes from. The sun is so massive that near its center the force of gravity is strong enough to crush its hydrogen atoms, causing the hydrogen, by a process we call "fusion," to turn into helium. (It is the same process that makes a hydrogen bomb explode.) The transformation releases tremendous amounts of energy that slowly work their way to the sun's surface where the energy radiates into space in all directions. An extremely small portion of this energy reaches the earth a little more than eight minutes after it leaves the sun.

The temperature at the sun's center is unimaginably hot: at least 35 million degrees Fahrenheit. This temperature lowers gradually as the energy moves outward until it is only about 10,000 degrees Fahrenheit at the sun's surface. That is still hot enough to vaporize an entire spaceship instantly.

Puzzling Question 9:

It is easy for astronomers to measure how fast the sun turns on its axis because its sunspots—vast whirlpools of gas that keep forming and vanishing on the sun's surface—appear as dark spots that last long enough for astronomers to follow their movement in a telescope and calculate how fast the sun is rotating.

At its equator the sun's surface rotates once in 24 days and 16 hours, only a few days less than it takes the moon to circle the earth. Consider the sun's surface nearer its poles. Does it rotate faster, slower, or at the same speed as the sun's surface at the equator?

Black dots are sunspots that have formed on the surface of the sun.

Puzzling Question 10:

Suppose you live on a street that runs exactly east and west. One day in September, when leaves are starting to turn color, you notice that the top half of a setting sun, like part of a huge red balloon, is exactly above the far west end of your street. What day of the month are you near?

Puzzling Question 11:

Spots on the sun go through repeating cycles of about 11 years. Their size and number vary irregularly from week to week, but on the average the time between periods when the spots are largest and most numerous is about 11 years. When this maximum period is reached, "magnetic storms" blow toward us from the sun. They cause the earth's northern and southern lights—the spectacular "aurora borealis" and "aurora australis" that shine in the night sky near the poles—to glow brighter than usual, and they play havoc with radio and other electronic communication.

Sunspots vary greatly in size. One enormous spot seen in 1947 was thirty times the size of the whole earth's surface! Most sunspots are much smaller than that and last only a few days or weeks, though some last several months. Occasionally one will remain visible for a year or longer.

The sun has a weak magnetic field with north and south magnetic poles like those on earth. What peculiar change happens to the sun's magnetic poles every 11 years when the sunspot cycle is at its maximum?

Puzzling Question 12:

When a new moon—that is, a moon that has waned until it is invisible—passes between the sun and earth, the moon will block off part or all of the sun's light and the event is called a solar eclipse. Total solar eclipses are much rarer than partial ones. It is only in certain parts of the earth that the moon's moving shadow will touch the earth's surface causing observers along this "path of totality" to see a total eclipse. The last one visible in the United States, you may recall, was early in 1970. During a total eclipse the sun is completely covered by the moon. Day turns to night, stars come out, dogs bark, birds go to roost. In times past people sometimes thought that the sun was vanishing forever and the world coming to an end.

Total eclipse of the sun.

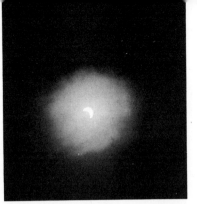

LEFT: *Partial solar eclipse with sun seen as a crescent.*
RIGHT: *Tiny crescents cast through the leaves of a tree during a partial solar eclipse.*

During a partial eclipse in summertime, when the sun becomes a crescent, sunlight will shine through the leaves of a tree and you will see hundreds of tiny little crescents of light on the ground, or perhaps on the side of a wall or house. Can you explain this strange phenomenon?

Puzzling Question 13:

During a total eclipse of the sun, just before the moon completely hides the sun's disk, brilliant little beads of light can be seen at the edge of the moon that is moving forward. The same beads appear later at the back edge of the moon when the moon starts to uncover the sun's disk. These are called "Baily's beads" after Francis Baily, an English astronomer, who noticed them during an eclipse in 1836.

Can you think what causes Baily's beads?

*Baily's Beads
seen during the eclipse of
February 25, 1952.*

Chapter 3 | THE MOON

The moon, earth's nearest neighbor in space, has a mean distance of about 239,000 miles from the earth, but its orbit is elliptical enough to make the distance vary from 221,463 to 252,710 miles. Its diameter of 2,160 miles is a little less than one-fourth the earth's, and its volume is about one fiftieth.

It takes the moon 27 days, 7 hours and 43 minutes to make a complete trip around the earth. This is called a "sidereal month." Because the earth is at the same time moving around the sun, the moon has to travel a trifle farther each time to bring the earth, sun and moon into the same relative positions as before. The time between two full moons, therefore, is longer than a sidereal month. It is 29 days, 12 hours and 44 minutes, almost as long as each of our calendar months except February. Astronomers call that period a "lunar month." Our word "month" is named for the moon. (It really should be called a "moonth.") Since the first day of the week,

28

This beautiful view of a full moon was taken from the Apollo 11 spacecraft on the return voyage from its moon landing, at a distance of 10,000 nautical miles.

Sunday, is named for the sun, it was only natural that the week's second day, Monday, should be named after what to us is the second most important object in the sky.

As the moon goes around the earth, the sun shines on it from different angles so that we see the moon slowly wax (more and more of it becomes bright) and wane (less and less of it is bright) from night to night. These are called the "phases" of the moon. When the

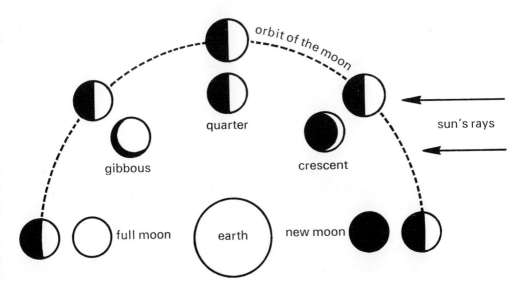

The phases of the moon. The outer spheres indicate the portion of the moon being lit by the sun's rays. The inner spheres indicate how that illumination is seen from the earth.

illuminated side of the moon is directly opposite the earth, the moon is completely dark and we call it "new." A thin crescent then forms and gradually grows thicker until exactly half the moon is illuminated. This is known as a "quarter moon." The bright portion continues to expand, creating a fat "gibbous moon." Finally, the entire disk is shining and we say the moon is "full." The moon then begins to wane, going slowly through these same phases in reverse order until it is new again.

Which is the more useful to mankind, the sun or the moon? This question is the basis of a joke that physicist George Gamow tells in his excellent book, *The Birth and Death of the Sun*. A philosopher, writes Gamow, once answered the question by saying that the moon is the more useful. Why? Because it gives light at night when it is needed, whereas the sun shines only during the day when it is light anyway!

We all know that the moon has no atmosphere or life, and that it is pocked by millions of craters of all sizes, most of which were undoubtedly produced by meteorites. Because the moon has no air to burn up meteors, even the smallest hit the moon's surface. The moon does not, of course, produce light of its own. Moonlight is merely reflected sunlight. "The moon's an arrant thief," was how Shakespeare put it, "and her pale fire she snatches from the sun."

It won't be long until people will be living on the moon for long periods, in an artificial atmosphere inside some type of protective dome or moonhouse. Our next step outward from the earth then surely will be to Mars.

The moon's surface is covered by millions of craters of various sizes. In the center of the picture is the Crater Lalande, a proposed site for future moon landings.

Puzzling Question 14:

The moon is the major cause of tides. Its gravity, sometimes assisted by the sun's gravity, pulls the water of our seas upward in a bulge about a foot or two high. As the earth turns, this "high tide" flows around the globe.

Not many people are aware that at the same time there is a high tide in oceans that are on the same side of the earth as the moon, there also is a high tide on the side directly *opposite* the moon. Can you explain the cause of this peculiar second high tide?

Puzzling Question 15:

As the astronaut walked cautiously over the moon's rugged surface, he looked up and saw thousands of stars twinkling brightly in the black night sky. To the west, a few wispy clouds were floating, and a light breeze was blowing moon-dust against the glass front of his helmet. A loud banging sound made him turn around to see what had happened. His companion had just split a large moon rock in half by hitting it with a hammer. In the east, the earth was almost "new"—hanging low in the sky like a cutting from a gigantic bluish-white fingernail. Inside the arms of the earth's shining crescent he could see several small stars.

How many scientific "howlers" can you find in the story quoted above?

Puzzling Question 16:

As the moon circles the earth it always keeps the same face toward us (except for a slight wobbling from side to side, known as the moon's "libration"). This is why it was not until space probes and space ships began traveling around the moon that we were able to photograph the side that had never before been seen from earth.

When the moon has made one complete trip around the earth, how many times has it rotated on its own axis?

Puzzling Question 17:

When the moon is almost new—that is, when it is an extremely thin crescent of light—you often can see faintly the rest of the moon's disk. In olden times people used to describe this by saying you could see the "old moon in the new moon's arms." To superstitious sailors the sight was considered a bad omen. Perhaps you remember from school this stanza from the old English ballad, *Sir Patrick Spens:*

> *Late, late yestreen I saw the new moone,*
> *Wi the auld moone in hir arme,*
> *And I feir, I feir, my deir master,*
> *That we will cum to harme.*

Where does the light come from that enables us to see the old moon in the arms of a new moon?

"The old moon in the new moon's arms." Bright, slender crescent, the "new moon," embraces the more dimly lit portion of the moon.

Puzzling Question 18:

Imagine a time in the future when a colony of men and women are living on the moon in a base supplied with air and heat so that they do not have to wear cumbersome space suits. In the colony is an athlete who on earth can jump over a bar six feet high, but no higher. The moon's gravity is one-sixth the strength of the earth's. This means that an object tossed straight up on the moon will go six times as high as it will on earth if thrown upward with the same force.

In view of all this, can the athlete on the moon jump over a bar 36 feet high?

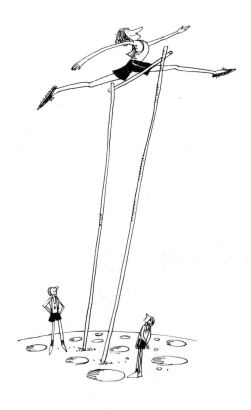

Chapter 4 | THE OTHER PLANETS

Our solar system consists of the sun, the nine planets and their moons, and an unknown number of asteroids and comets. In ancient and medieval times only the five planets that are visible to the naked eye—Mercury, Venus, Mars, Jupiter and Saturn—were known. The

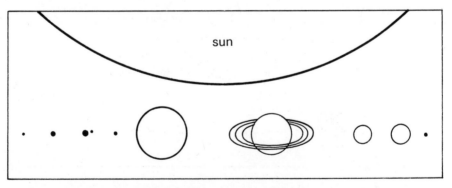

The relative sizes of the sun and the planets. From left to right the planets are, according to increasing distance from the sun: Mercury, Venus, Earth (with moon), Mars, Jupiter, Saturn, Uranus, Neptune, Pluto.

three outermost planets—Uranus, Neptune and Pluto—
were not known before 1781 when Uranus was discovered. Are there other planets beyond the orbit of Pluto?
There could be. No one really knows. A small planet

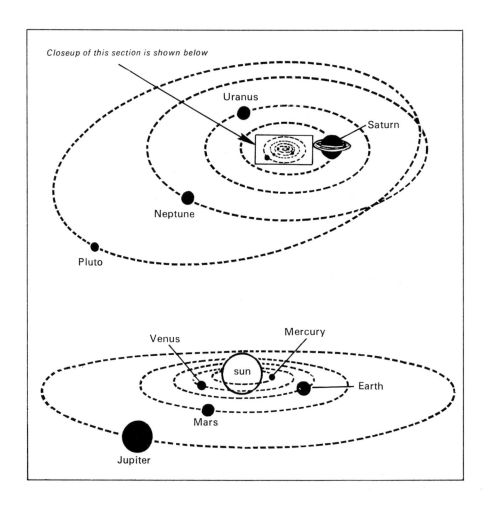

*The orbits of the planets are slightly elliptical in shape. Here,
the orbits are shown according to their relative distances
from the sun.*

beyond Pluto probably could not be seen through even our best telescopes.

The name "planet" comes from the Greek word for "wanderer." The planets were so called because, unlike the fixed stars, they wander across the sky in erratic, looping paths that were hard to account for until astronomers finally became convinced that the sun, not the earth, was the center of the solar system.

The planets do not move in perfect circles, as Galileo believed, but in slightly elliptical paths called orbits. These orbits are almost circular but not quite. Mercury and Pluto, the planets nearest and farthest from the sun, have paths that depart the most from a circle. Venus' orbit is the closest to a true circle. If you were to draw the orbit of Venus to scale on a sheet of typewriter paper you would be unable to detect by measuring it that it was not a circle.

Puzzling Question 19:

This and the next three questions are word puzzles about the planets that you may find amusing. We will get back to some serious problems in Question 23.

What is the meaning of the following series of letters?

MVEMJSUNP

The underlined word, SUN, is a clue.

Puzzling Question 20:

Can you find three words in the following sentence each with letters that can be rearranged to spell the name of a planet?

37

"When he saw the big rams running toward him, his heart started to beat wildly and he began waving his arms for help."

Puzzling Question 21:

What two planets have names such that, if you change just one letter of either name, you can rearrange all the letters to spell the name of the other planet?

Puzzling Question 22:

One time, while riding an airplane, I found myself seated between two ladies. One said she came from Mars, the other said she came from Venus. Were they telling the truth?

MERCURY

Mercury is the planet closest to the sun. It is the smallest planet and the fastest moving. Because of its speed the Greeks named it for their god Hermes (Mercury to the Romans), the messenger of the gods whose winged feet enabled him to travel rapidly through the sky. The little planet has a diameter of about 3,000 miles. It has no atmosphere and, because it is so close to the sun, it is difficult to see without a telescope. Like Venus and our moon, it goes through "phases," waxing and waning in brightness as more or less of its surface

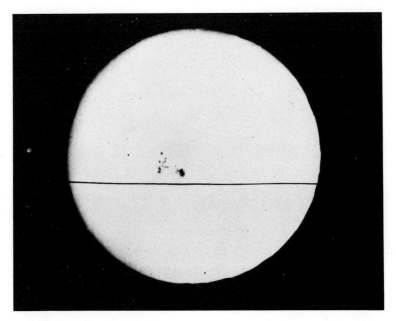

Mercury, the small black dot at the bottom, is in transit across the sun, moving to the right. The black horizontal line is caused by the camera; black dots above this line are sunspots.

is illuminated by the sun. It takes Mercury 88 days to make one trip around the sun.

About thirteen or fourteen times a century, Mercury's path, as seen from earth, takes it directly across the sun's disk. This is called a "transit." During the transit Mercury appears in telescopes (with suitable filters to cut down the sun's brightness) as a tiny black dot moving slowly in front of the sun. Transits of Mercury can take place only in May or November. The last one took place on May 9, 1970. There will be no more May transits this century, but November transits will occur in 1973, 1986 and 1999.

40

Puzzling Question 23:

For 75 years astronomers believed that Mercury always kept the same face toward the sun, just as our moon keeps the same face toward the earth. If so, Mercury would be too hot on one side and too cold on the other to support life. However, between the two sides there might be a belt of perpetual twilight in which the temperature could be mild enough to allow life to flourish. Many science fiction stories have been written about this Twilight Zone.

Does Mercury have a Twilight Zone?

VENUS

Venus is sometimes called the "morning star" and sometimes the "evening star" because it is so near the sun that we see it only at sunrise and sunset. Like Mercury and our moon, it goes through phases. When

Venus, during five of its phases.

Venus is "full," it glows like a big star near the horizon. The Greeks named it Aphrodite after their goddess of love and beauty whom the Romans called Venus.

Venus resembles Mercury in having no moon, but unlike Mercury it does have an atmosphere. The atmosphere is hot and dense. Its exact nature is still unknown, but space probes have found that it is about 95 per cent carbon dioxide mixed with small amounts of other gases. Above Venus' air there are yellowish clouds, perhaps composed of dust or ice crystals or particles of some other substance. These clouds are so thick that they have never parted to allow astronomers even a fleeting glimpse of the surface. Recent radar observations, however, suggest that Venus may have at least two mountain ranges, each roughly the size of our Rocky Mountains. Little else is known about the planet's surface.

The thick, swirling Venusian clouds allow the sun's radiation to get through and heat the planet's surface, but the same clouds prevent the heat from escaping. This is called the "greenhouse effect" because the heavy glass of a greenhouse traps heat inside the house in a similar way. As a result, the surface of Venus is too hot and dry to support life as we know it. In December, 1970, the Russian craft, Venera 7, made a soft landing on Venus and broadcast data for more than twenty minutes. It was the first time that scientific information had been sent to the earth from the surface of another planet. The information indicated a surface temperature on Venus' dark side of 847-923 degrees Fahrenheit and a crushing atmospheric pressure ninety times that of the earth. Some astronomers have suggested that there may be small living organisms of some sort floating in the cooler atmosphere above the surface.

Venus is the planet nearest in size to the earth. Its diameter of about 7,500 miles is only a few hundred miles less than the earth's. Of all the planets Venus is the one that swings closest to us. On rare occasions—much less often than Mercury—Venus makes a transit across the sun's disk. Venus' last transit was in 1882. There will not be another until June 8, 2004.

Puzzling Question 24:

The true nature of Venus' rotation was not discovered until 1965 when astronomers bounced radar waves from opposite sides of Venus to determine exactly how fast it turns on its axis. The results were astonishing. Do you know what they were?

| MARS

Although Mars is considerably smaller than the earth, it is the one other planet most likely to have some form of life. It is generally cold on Mars's surface—far below freezing at night—but not too cold for life. Mars has a thin atmosphere that is mostly carbon dioxide, with almost no oxygen or water vapor. No trace of nitrogen has yet been found on Mars, though some nitrogen is probably there.

The reason for Mars's thin atmosphere is its low gravity—about a third that of the earth. This is too weak to keep oxygen and nitrogen from evaporating into outer space. On the other hand, Mars does have winter polar caps, believed to be frost coatings of dry ice (frozen carbon dioxide), that disappear in Mars's spring. The melting of those caps could provide enough water to support a primitive, perhaps microscopic, form of plant

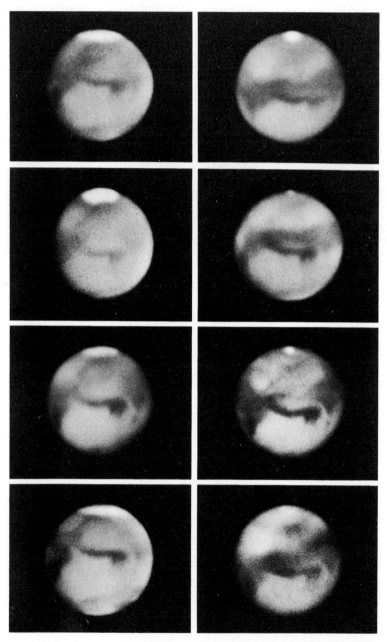

Mars's polar caps (bright spots on top of each sphere), as they begin to melt in the spring (4 photos on left) and then slowly disappear in the summer (4 photos on the right).

or animal life, or something in-between that we wouldn't know whether to call plant or animal. Dark patches on Mars's surface change color with the seasons. Some astronomers believe this may indicate vegetation, but the changes of color could also be caused by geologic processes which we will not understand until our astronauts explore the planet.

Mars's diameter is about 4,200 miles. Like the earth, Mars is flattened slightly at its poles. Its day is almost the same length as ours, 24 hours, 37 minutes and 22 seconds, but its year (the time it takes to orbit the sun) is almost twice as long—687 earth days. It was because of its reddish appearance, which suggested blood, that the ancients named the ruddy planet after Ares or Mars, the god of war.

Mars has two small moons. They were not detected until 1877 although more than a century before this date, in 1726, in fact, Jonathan Swift, in his book, *Gulliver's Travels,* made the remarkable guess that Mars had two moons. He even came fairly close to guessing their actual orbital periods!

This is how Gulliver put it in Chapter 3 of his *Voyage to Laputa:*

> They [the Laputans] have likewise discovered two lesser stars, or satellites, which revolve about Mars, whereof the innermost . . . revolves in the space of ten hours, and the latter in twenty-one and an half. . . .

Mars's two moons are now called Phobos and Deimos after the horses which the ancients believed drew Mars's chariot. Latest observations suggest that Phobos is lopsided, with diameters of about fourteen and eleven miles, and that Deimos has a diameter of about five miles.

Phobos is the only known moon in the solar system that whirls around a planet at a *faster* speed than the planet's rotation. Indeed, Phobos speeds around Mars three times for each single rotation of the planet. Although Phobos moves in the same direction that the planet rotates, astronauts on Mars would see Phobos rise in the *west,* remain in the sky only about 5½ hours, then set in the *east!* (Deimos rises in the east and stays above Mars's horizon about two days.) This peculiar behavior of Phobos, and other unusual facts about the two moons, led a Russian astronomer to suggest seriously, in 1950, that the moons could be space stations built by Martians. At some time in the far distant past, he argued, perhaps Martians had constructed them as launching platforms to escape from their planet when it became too arid to support them. Most astronomers think that this is not very likely.

Puzzling Question 25:
You have surely heard about the famous so-called "canals" of Mars, mentioned so often in science fiction stories about the planet. What is the latest information about these canals?

JUPITER

Jupiter, named for the chief god of the Romans (their equivalent of the Greek god Zeus), is the largest of the planets. It is so large that all the other planets, pushed together into a ball, would still be smaller than Jupiter.

It is flattened at its poles so much more than Mars and the earth that in a telescope it has the shape of a grapefruit. At its equator the planet's diameter is 88,000 miles, but its pole-to-pole diameter is 6,000 miles less. This equatorial bulging is caused by the planet's unusually rapid rotation: once in a little less than ten hours. A Jovian year is almost twelve earth years.

Jupiter's atmosphere, perhaps thousands of miles deep, is made up of such gases as hydrogen, helium, methane and ammonia. The planet's fast spin causes the atmosphere to form a dozen or so bands, all roughly parallel to the equator, that are varying tints of rust, yellow, orange, brown and white. The bands alter from time to time in number, width, color, and even in the speeds with which they rotate. Sometimes greenish or bluish patches appear for a while on the bands, only to vanish later.

The thick, turbulent atmosphere of Jupiter is subject to horrendous storms accompanied by violent outbursts of energy that can be detected in our radio telescopes. Some astronomers believe that this crackling radio noise comes from enormous lightning bolts on the planet. Other astronomers believe the noise is produced by the eruptions of Jovian volcanoes.

The depth of Jupiter's atmosphere has prevented any glimpse of its surface. Many experts hold the view that Jupiter has no "surface" at all. It may be that the atmosphere simply gets denser at greater depths, gradually turning from gas to liquid, and that the liquid portion of the planet, at still greater depths, gradually becomes solid. Perhaps there is an inner core heated to a molten state by the enormous pressures created by Jupiter's gravity. If Jupiter does have a true solid surface on which an astronaut could stand, he would have difficulty staying on his feet. A 180-pound man on earth would weigh about 470 pounds on Jupiter.

How hot or cold is Jupiter's surface, assuming it has one? This, too, is a much debated question. For many years astronomers assumed that, because of its great distance from the sun, the planet would be far below freezing, much too cold to support life. Recent observations have suggested, however, that the "greenhouse effect" (mentioned earlier in connection with Venus) could make Jupiter's surface too *hot* for life as we know it on earth. It may turn out that, if there is no genuine surface, the temperature is very cold at the top of the planet's atmosphere, then gets progressively warmer toward the interior. If so, there may be a zone, possibly even a solid one, where the climate is temperate enough to permit life to have developed, an exciting possibility that had not seemed likely to astronomers until quite recently.

Jupiter has twelve moons, more than any other planet. The four largest—Io, Europa, Ganymede and Callisto— were first seen by Galileo in 1610 when he peered at

Four of the brighter moons of Jupiter are seen in three different positions as they revolve around the planet.

Jupiter through a crude telescope he had built himself. (Galileo did not invent the telescope, as is often believed. Telescopes had previously been sold in Europe as toys. What Galileo did was to construct a much better telescope than anyone had built before.) You can see Jupiter's four largest moons today with a pair of strong binoculars. The moons of Jupiter played a major role in the first measurement of the speed of light. In 1675 Olaus Römer, a Danish astronomer, used the orbital periods of Jupiter's moons to determine how fast light traveled.

The most distant four moons, all about 15 million miles from Jupiter, circle the planet the "wrong way." Viewed from above the planet's north pole, they revolve clockwise instead of counterclockwise as do all the planets and all other moons in the solar system except (as we shall see) one of Saturn's and one of Neptune's.

Puzzling Question 26:
What is Jupiter's Great Red Spot?

SATURN

Saturn, with its beautiful rings, is the most dazzling of all planets when seen through a telescope. We will come to the rings in a moment. First, a few basic facts.

Saturn is the second largest planet, and it is named for the god who was the father of Jupiter. Saturn spins so fast—once in a little more than ten hours—that it bulges almost as much as Jupiter at its equator. From

Saturn and its rings.

pole to pole its diameter is about 67,000 miles, but at the equator the diameter is more than 71,000 miles. Saturn's year is 29½ earth years.

Like the other three of the larger planets—Jupiter, Neptune and Uranus—Saturn has a much lower density than the earth and the other small planets. (The density of an object is its weight per unit of volume.) It is the only planet with a density less than water. This means that Saturn actually would *float* on water—if there were an ocean anywhere big enough to hold it.

Saturn's atmosphere is thousands of miles deep. It is probably similar to Jupiter's in its chemical composition. The rapid whirling of the planet forms bands of clouds, as on Jupiter, though the bands are less clearly visible to us. No one knows what its surface is like or whether it has one. Like Jupiter, it may simply get denser with depth.

Saturn has ten moons. The tenth, Janus, was not discovered until 1966. The ninth moon, Phoebe (found in 1898) revolves the "wrong way" like Jupiter's four outer moons. Titan, about the same size as Mercury, is the only moon in the solar system known to have an atmosphere. The atmosphere is probably methane, which can be used as rocket fuel. This has led Arthur C. Clarke, the well-known science fiction author, to speculate that some day our astronauts may use Titan as a stopover base for refueling their spaceships.

Japetus, another moon of Saturn, has the curious property of becoming six times brighter on one side of its orbit than on the other. No one knows why. If you have seen the motion picture *2001: A Space Odyssey,* or read Clarke's novel based on the picture (in turn based on an earlier short story by Clarke), you may recall the important role played in the story by Japetus: It is an artificial satellite built by extraterrestrial beings to receive a signal from a slab placed on our moon, and to receive the earth's spaceship when it arrives at Saturn.

Saturn's wondrous rings were first seen by Galileo in 1610 when he also saw the four largest moons of Jupiter. His telescope was too poor, unfortunately, for him to recognize them as rings. He thought Saturn had two smaller bodies, one bulging out on each side. Later astronomers, with better telescopes, recognized them as three distinct rings. The inner ring is too faint to be seen without a powerful telescope. It is about 11,000 miles wide. Then there is a gap of about a thousand miles of space that separates the inner ring from a bright central ring, 18,000 miles wide. Beyond a much larger second gap of about 1,500 miles, called the Cassini Division, is the outer ring, 12,000 miles wide. In 1969 a fourth ring, almost touching the planet and very faint, was observed by a French astronomer.

51

The four rings girdle Saturn's equator. They are semi-transparent (stars can sometimes be seen through them) and they are probably composed of particles about the size of sand grains. Most astronomers believe they are particles of dust and some type of ice. There is no agreement on how the rings were formed. Perhaps a satellite exploded from violent tidal forces when it got too close to the planet. Perhaps they are ancient particles that never congealed to form a satellite. If the last theory is true, it is possible that other planets, including the earth, may once have had rings like Saturn's.

After Galileo proudly announced his discovery that Saturn had two smaller bodies on each side, he was amazed and embarrassed to find that two years later both bodies had entirely vanished! The planet was a bare sphere. There was no sign of anything else.

> What [Galileo wrote] is to be said concerning so strange a metamorphosis? Are the two lesser stars consumed like sunspots? Have they vanished and suddenly fled? Has Saturn, perhaps, devoured his own children? Or were these appearances indeed illusion and fraud, with which the telescope has so long deceived me, as well as many others to whom I have shown it? . . . I do not know what to say in a case so surprising, so unlooked for, so novel. The shortness of the time, the unexpected nature of the event, the weakness of my understanding, and the fear of being mistaken, have greatly confounded me.

Puzzling Question 27:

But poor Galileo was not mistaken. Can you guess what had happened to make the rings of Saturn disappear so mysteriously?

URANUS, NEPTUNE AND PLUTO

Uranus is not visible without a telescope unless one has extremely sharp vision and the night sky is unusually clear. It was not known to be a planet until 1781. The discoverer was not a professional astronomer but a British musician, William Herschel, who had made astronomy his hobby. He discovered the planet with a small telescope he had built himself. The planet was named after the Greek god of the heavens. (The name is usually mispronounced. The accent should be on the first syllable, not the second.)

Little is known about Uranus except its diameter

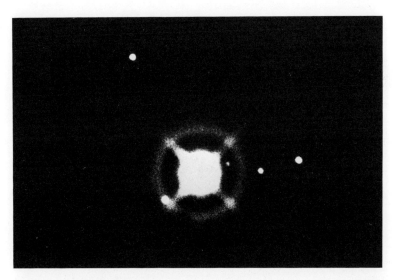

Uranus and its five known satellites. Miranda, the smallest of the satellites and the last to be discovered, is the small white object inside the ring. The ring (called a halation ring) is caused by the camera lens.

(about 29,500 miles), its rotation period (like Saturn's, a little more than 10 hours), and its period of revolution around the sun (84 earth years). Uranus' most peculiar feature is that its axis of rotation is so nearly on the plane of the solar system that either end can be called north. For this reason one cannot really say in which direction it rotates. It has five moons all revolving around its equator in the same direction that the planet spins. Miranda (named after the heroine of Shakespeare's *Tempest*) was the last to be discovered. It is the smallest of Uranus' moons and the one closest to the planet.

Neptune and Pluto are visible only in telescopes. Neptune, named for the Roman god of the sea, was discovered in 1845 after astronomers suspected it was there because they had noticed an irregularity in the path of Uranus that could only be caused by the gravitational in-

Neptune and its two satellites. Triton, the larger of the two satellites, is the large bright spot in the lower left corner, and Nereid, the smaller satellite, is shown by the arrow.

Pluto (arrow) is seen in two different positions among the stars in a 24-hour period.

fluence of a more distant planet. Neptune has a diameter of about 27,000 miles, a rotation period of almost 16 hours, and a year equal to about 165 earth years. Triton, the larger of its two moons, circles "backward" around the planet.

Pluto, named after the Roman god of the underworld, was not discovered until 1930. It is so far from the sun (over three billion miles) that it receives almost no heat or light, and is surely a desolate, perpetually frozen planet. It revolves around the sun once in about 248 earth years. Its size is not accurately known. At first it was thought to be almost as big as the earth, but later estimates make its diameter closer to 3,600 miles, less than half that of the earth's. Its rotation period is believed to be about six days.

Puzzling Question 28:

Is it possible that Pluto was once a moon of Neptune?

Chapter 5 | COMETS AND ASTEROIDS

COMETS

Comets are large chunks of rock, or gases frozen solid by the deep cold of outer space, that plunge into the center of the solar system, wheel around the sun, then go back into outer space again. Some travel elliptical paths that have been computed, enabling astronomers to predict when they will return. Other comets come and go, never to be seen again. Some astronomers believe that these one-visit comets have never been here before and never will come again. If so, they travel paths that are either parabolas or hyperbolas. (The ellipse, parabola and hyperbola are called "conic section" curves because they can be obtained by cutting a cone at various angles.) Other astronomers are convinced that *all* comets are part of our solar system, but that some have such enormously long elliptical orbits that it may take hundreds of years for them to return.

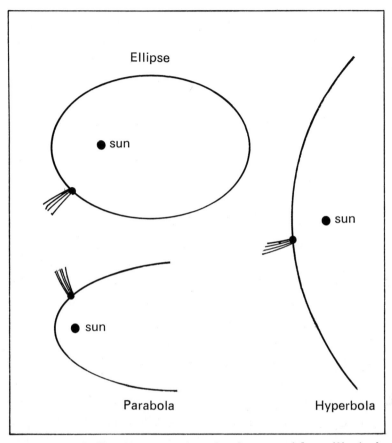

Ellipse

sun

Parabola

sun

Hyperbola

sun

Comets are believed to travel paths that are either elliptical, parabolic or hyperbolic.

There are two main theories about how comets are formed. According to one theory, as the sun moves through clouds of interstellar dust, its gravity pulls the particles together to form a dense stream that trails behind the sun like the wake of a ship. Occasionally, an enormous clump of particles is drawn toward the sun to become a comet. According to the rival theory, the sun's planets are surrounded by a permanent whirling cloud of particles containing billions of clumps, a cloud that extends halfway to the nearest star. Now and then the gravitational influence of nearby stars deflects the path of a clump, causing it to swing close to the sun and become visible on earth as a comet.

Some comets have been captured by the strong gravity of Jupiter. They go around the sun *and* Jupiter, their orbits entirely within the solar system. Other comets remain inside the solar system, but their orbits carry them out as far as the paths of Saturn, Uranus or Neptune.

Comets have no tails until they get close to the sun. The intense solar heat vaporizes portions of them, and the gas blows out to form a glowing, smokelike streamer. The tails vary enormously in size and shape. Sometimes they are short, sometimes hundreds of millions of miles long. Sometimes they are straight, sometimes curved. Some comets have two tails at the same time. Others never develop a tail. Because a comet loses part of its substance every time a tail is formed, it is sure to burn itself out eventually. That may happen after only fifty orbits, or it may happen after hundreds of orbits. In many cases what is left is a swarm of rocky pieces that roam space as a cloud of meteors.

The last spectacular comet appeared in 1882; it could be seen with the naked eye for several weeks. Since that time most comets have been too faint to be visible without a telescope. A famous large comet, called Halley's comet after a seventeenth-century English astronomer, Edmund Halley, belongs to the Jupiter family. It returns to the sun every 76 years. It was last seen in 1910, when the earth actually went through the tip of its tail. Halley's comet is not due back until 1986.

Puzzling Question 29:

The picture shows how the comet of 1882 appeared at Streatham, England, on November 4, at four in the morning. Can you tell from the drawing in which direction the comet is moving?

The Comet of 1882

ASTEROIDS

Concentrated primarily within the enormously vast gap between the orbits of Mars and Jupiter, there are hundreds of thousands of rocky objects called asteroids or planetoids. They come in all sizes and shapes ranging from the largest, Ceres (with a diameter of about 450 miles), down to pieces of rock too small to be detected from the earth.

Ceres was the first asteroid to be discovered (in 1801).

The second, Pallas, was found the following year. It is the second largest asteroid, with a diameter close to 300 miles.

There are many theories about how the asteroids originated. Some astronomers believe them to be the remnants of a planet that came so close to Jupiter that it was wrenched apart by Jovian gravity and broke into myriads of pieces. Others believe that the asteroids resulted from a collision between two or more small planets. Still others think the solar system originated in a swirling cloud of particles that once surrounded the sun, and that the asteroids are rocks that never came together to form a planet. In any case, the total mass of the asteroids is less than that of our moon.

The asteroids circle the sun in periods that vary from two to twelve years. Many of their orbits are steeply inclined to the "ecliptic"—the plane on which the earth revolves. Hidalgo, for instance, has an orbit tipped almost 45 degrees to the ecliptic.

Only one asteroid, Vesta—its diameter is about 250 miles—can be seen with the unaided eye. This is not because Vesta is so large or comes so near the earth, but because its surface reflects more light than other large asteroids. Astronomers do not know why, but probably it happens because Vesta has an unusually smooth surface. No asteroid is big enough to keep an atmosphere. On Ceres, the largest, a one hundred-pound boy would weigh less than four pounds. On smaller asteroids, an astronaut could easily jump off with enough velocity to escape into space and never come back.

Of special interest to astronomers are two groups of asteroids known as the "Trojan asteroids." They were given that name because each member of these groups that has been identified is named for a warrior in Homer's *Iliad,* an epic poem that tells of the famous Trojan War between Greece and Troy. To explain why the Trojan asteroids are of such importance we must go back to 1772 when a French mathematician and astronomer, Count Joseph Louis Lagrange, made an exciting discovery. He proved mathematically that two bodies (or groups of bodies) could circle the sun in such a way that they would always be at two corners of an equilateral triangle, with the sun situated at the

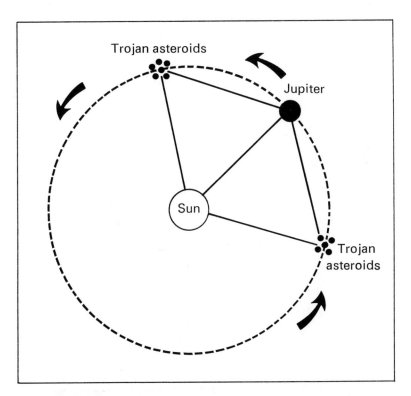

The Lagrangian points of Jupiter and the two groups of Trojan asteroids.

triangle's third corner. In other words, the triangular pattern would remain stable. It was no more than an oddity of mathematical astronomy until 1906 when astronomers found an asteroid, named Achilles, at a "Lagrangian point." The other two corners of the equilateral triangle are marked by the sun and Jupiter.

Since 1906 more than a dozen asteroids have been found at Jupiter's two Lagrangian points, one clump keeping in front of Jupiter, the other trailing behind. As shown in the drawing, while Jupiter goes around the sun, these asteroid clumps remain permanently locked at the corners of two giant equilateral triangles. They provide a dramatic proof of the correctness of Lagrange's equations.

Puzzling Question 30:

Is it possible that some day the earth might collide with a large asteroid?

Puzzling Question 31:

The 694th asteroid to be discovered was named Ekard by its discoverer. (Whoever finds a new asteroid is permitted to give it whatever name he wishes. One is called Chicago, and another, Marlene, is named for the famous motion picture star, Marlene Dietrich.) Ekard is an odd name. Can you guess what it stands for?

Chapter 6 | SPACE FLIGHT

A few years before the Wright brothers made their first successful airplane flight there were many intelligent people, including scientists, who said flatly that workable flying machines would never be built. Simon Newcomb, an American astronomer, was particularly scornful. "Quite likely," he said, "the most effective flying machine would be one carried by a vast number of little birds."

The same lack of imagination prompted many scientists to make equally embarrassing predictions about the impossibility of space flight. The famous University of Chicago astronomer, Forest Ray Moulton, in a once much-used college textbook, *Astronomy* (1931), page 296, wrote:

> Many a story has been written of some miraculous journey to the moon or Mars. . . . There is no hope, however, that such a wish will ever be realized. The difficulty of escaping Earth's gravity is insuperable; the problem of directing a journey through celestial spaces and that of descending gently to rest on the surface of another gravitating body are equally formidable. Only those who are unfamiliar with the physical forces involved believe that such adventures will ever pass beyond the realms of fancy.

The great early writers of science fiction, however, never doubted for a moment that spaceships of earth would some day explore the moon and the planets. Jules Verne's popular novel, *All Around the Moon* (1870), a sequel to his earlier novel about the building of the spaceship, told of a flight around the moon by three men in a ship launched from Tampa, Florida, not far from where our Cape Kennedy Space Center now stands. The command module of Apollo 11, which carried our astronauts to the first moon landing, was named *Columbia* after the *Columbiad,* Verne's imaginary ship. The *Columbiad* even splashed down in the Pacific where its astronauts were picked up by a United States vessel.

64

These two drawings from the original edition of Jules Verne's All Around the Moon *show the spaceship, the* Columbiad, *as it is about to land on the moon (left), and the ship and its three passengers after they have landed. It is interesting to compare this 19th-century artist's conception of a moon landing with a photograph of the actual landing of the Lunar Module "Intrepid" during the voyage of Apollo 12 (see page 66).*

There is no need here to go over the familiar, dramatic story of modern space flight. Instead, I will quote some passages from *The World Set Free,* a novel by H. G. Wells, another famous pioneer writer of science fiction. The novel was published in 1914. It is Wells's most prophetic work of fiction because it tells of the splitting of the atom and how this knowledge was used to build what Wells called "atomic bombs"—bombs that were dropped in a devastating war that Wells imagined occurring near the middle of the twentieth century. Here are some lines from the novel's final chapter. They are a marvelous anticipation of the space age, an age which arrived much *earlier* than Wells expected.

"This round planet is no longer chained to us like the ball of a galley slave. . . . In a little while men who will know how to bear the strange gravitations, the altered pressures, the attenuated, unfamiliar gases, and all the fearful strangeness of space, will be venturing out from this earth. This ball will be no longer enough for us; our spirit will reach out . . ."

And then Karenin stood up. He walked a few paces along the terrace and remained for a time gazing up at that great silver disk, that silvery shield that must needs be man's first conquest in outer space. . . .

This first conquest, the conquest of the moon, has now been made decades ahead of Wells's schedule. It will not be long until our astronauts will be exploring Mars and Venus, then other planets of the solar system. Who can say what surprises are in store for us, or that man will not some day be visiting even stranger planets that belong to other suns?

The second moon landing, Apollo 12, is about to take place as the Lunar Module "Intrepid," with astronauts Charles Conrad, Jr., and Alan Bean aboard, descends toward the landing site. The Lunar Module has separated from the Command Module, the "Yankee Clipper," containing astronaut Richard Gordon.

Puzzling Question 32:

Inertia is the tendency of a body at rest to stay at rest or of a body in motion to continue moving in a straight line unless acted upon by an outside force. Suppose an astronaut, in zero gravity, uncovers a glass of water and wants to empty it quickly into the air. Describe three different ways he can do this by using the water's inertia.

Puzzling Question 33:

Explain three ways artificial gravity can be created inside a moving spaceship.

Puzzling Question 34:

Will a candle burn in zero gravity inside a spaceship containing an atmosphere like that on earth?

Puzzling Question 35:

An astronaut takes a long trip away from earth while his twin brother, of course of exactly the same age, stays at home. When the traveling twin returns will the ages of the two brothers be the same?

Puzzling Question 36:

In Jules Verne's novel about a trip around the moon, mentioned earlier, the spaceship *Columbiad* is shot from a gigantic cannon in Florida. It travels around the moon and back without any propulsion system. On the way to the moon, Verne's space travelers find their weight slowly getting less and less as they get farther from the earth. When their ship reaches a point in space at which the pull of the earth exactly balances the pull of the moon, there is zero gravity inside the ship.

What big scientific mistake did Verne make?

Puzzling Question 37:

Verne made another blooper in his novel about a trip around the moon. During the voyage the space travelers toss out of their spaceship's window the body of a dog named Satellite, which has been killed by the violent launching of the ship. Hours later they see the dog's body still moving alongside the ship.

What is wrong about this incident?

Puzzling Question 38:

In zero gravity what happens to the air space inside a closed, half-filled bottle of water?

Puzzling Question 39:

Two spaceships speed toward each other, one at 9,000 miles per hour, the other at 21,000 miles per hour. They start 15,537 miles apart in space. How far apart are they one minute before they pass each other?

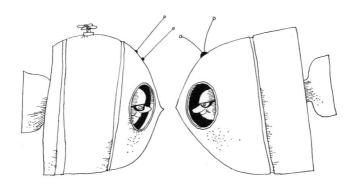

Puzzling Question 40:

If you are in a canoe and have lost your paddles, it is possible to start the canoe moving through the water by the following unusual method. Attach a rope to the back end of the canoe. By repeatedly jerking the rope toward the front of the boat you can start the canoe moving slowly forward. As long as you keep yanking, the boat will keep moving.

Could such a method be applied to a spaceship marooned in outer space?

Puzzling Question 41:

If an astronaut, unprotected by a spacesuit, were suddenly to step out of his spaceship into the vacuum of space, would he explode from the pressures inside his body?

ANSWERS

Chapter 1: THE EARTH

1. No, you would not. High as our mountains seem to us (some are higher than five miles), and deep as our valleys and ocean beds are (some run deeper than six miles), the earth is so much larger in comparison to those heights and depths that if it were the size of an ivory billiard ball it would feel even *smoother* than such a ball.

2. In a deep mine your weight (the pull on you of the earth's gravity) would be a trifle less than on the earth's surface. The reason is that there is a smaller amount of earth below you to pull you downward, and some earth above you to pull you *up*. The deeper you go, the weaker the downward force. At the center of the earth, if the mine went that deep, you would weigh nothing at all.

3. A man sitting on a horse is higher above the earth's surface than when he is standing on the ground, so he weighs a tiny amount less.

4. The problem of what would happen if you fell through a tube that went straight through the earth's center was correctly answered by Galileo. Ignoring friction on the sides, and air resistance, you would fall faster and faster until you reached your greatest speed—about five miles per second—at the center of the earth. Although the pull of gravity gets weaker as you get closer to the earth's center, the inertia of your falling body—its property of keeping on going in the same di-

71

rection—combined with the constant tug of gravity, causes your speed to accelerate (continually increase) until you reach the center. Once you pass the center, your speed starts *decreasing* because now most of the earth is behind you and exerting a stronger pull than the portion of the earth ahead of you. Your velocity slows to zero just as you arrive at the tube's other opening.

Unless you grabbed the edge of the tube (or someone grabbed you) gravity would pull you down into the tube again and you would fall back the other way. Under ideal conditions you would oscillate back and forth forever, making each round trip in about 84 minutes.

5. Gravity trains would indeed work. Of course friction on the rails and air resistance would slow such a train down, but if these and other interfering forces are neglected, a train could travel through a straight tunnel from, say, Los Angeles to London, powered by nothing except gravity.

Study the picture and you will see that during the first half of the train's trip it is rolling downhill (toward the earth's center). Like someone falling through the earth, the train acquires enough speed to coast back up the other half of the tube. Strangely enough, it turns out that the time it would take a train to make such a trip (under ideal, frictionless conditions) is exactly the same as the time it would take a person to fall through the earth in one direction—about 42 minutes. This time is the same no matter how long or short the straight tunnel.

Like the tube through the earth, underground railways of this kind have been described in many science fiction stories. In recent years modified forms of such transportation, using gravity to help start and stop underground trains, have been seriously proposed by engineers.

6. No. This is an old superstition with no basis in fact. The same applies to the similar belief that stars can be seen in daylight by looking up a tall chimney. Since stars are visible only at night, it seemed reasonable to suppose that if you looked up a dark well or chimney it would be the same as looking at a night sky. But of course it isn't. The small patch of day sky around a star is just as bright when viewed through a long, dark well or chimney as it is when you are standing in an open field.

7. Ten pounds. Did it occur to you that you actually can *do* this experiment? Just turn a table upside down! According to Newton's law of gravity, any two objects attract each other with equal force. Therefore, if the earth pulls the table with a force of ten pounds, the table is simultaneously pulling the earth with a force of ten pounds.

The situation is like that of an enormous iron ball floating in space and attached to a cork by a rubber band. If you stretch the band an equal amount at each end and let go, the cork will be the object that moves. The iron ball is so massive that its movement will be undetectable, but nevertheless it *will* move a tiny bit. The attractive force created by the stretched elastic band (which corresponds to gravity) is exactly the same in both directions.

8. As the earth plunges through a swarm of meteors, its "face," the side toward the earth's direction of movement around the sun, will hit more meteors than its opposite side. From sunset to midnight you are on the earth's *back* side. From midnight to sunrise you are on its *front* side. In other words, you see more shooting stars in the early morning hours for the same reason your face gets wetter than the back of your head when you run through falling raindrops on a windless day.

Chapter 2: THE SUN

9. Curiously, the sun's surface rotates at different speeds. Near the poles it takes about ten days longer for the surface to make a single rotation than for the surface near the equator. Astronomers do not yet know why.

10. Because the earth's axis is tilted at an angle to the plane on which it revolves around the sun, the sun appears to travel across the sky along a path called "the ecliptic" that varies during the year in its distance north or south. Only twice a year does the sun rise and set at spots that are precisely east and west. When this happens, a day (sunrise to sunset) is exactly as long as a night (sunset to sunrise). The two dates are called "equinoxes." The vernal or spring equinox occurs on or near March 21. The autumnal equinox occurs on or near September 23. It is this last date that answers the question asked in the problem.

The day when the sun sets as far north as possible is called the winter "solstice." This day falls about De-

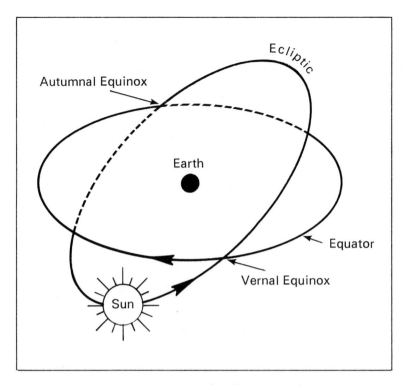

The apparent path traced out by the sun as it moves across the sky determines the plane of the Ecliptic as it crosses the plane of the earth's orbit. The points of intersection of the two orbits are called equinoxes.

cember 22, the time when the day is shortest. The summer solstice, which falls about June 22, is the time when the day is longest. We say "about" in giving these dates because, like the equinoxes, the exact date varies slightly from year to year. This is because our years vary in length, each leap year being one day longer than other years.

11. For some strange reason, not yet understood, the sun's magnetic poles do a complete flip-flop when the sunspot cycle is at its maximum. The north pole be-

comes south pole and vice versa! Because of this switching of poles, a full sunspot cycle is said to last 22 years. For half that time the north pole is at one end of the axis of rotation, and half that time it is at the other end.

12. The leaves of a tree create hundreds of small holes through which sunlight passes. These holes act like the hole of a pinhole camera, producing upside-down images of the sun on the ground or on a wall or on the side of a house (see diagram below). Normally we are not aware of these images because they are merely round blobs of light. During a partial eclipse of the sun, however, we see the images as little crescents.

A pinhole in a sheet of cardboard furnishes a safe way to view a solar eclipse. It is dangerous to look at an eclipse directly, even when it is total, because of invisible solar radiation that can do permanent damage to your eyes. If you stick a pin through a large piece of card-

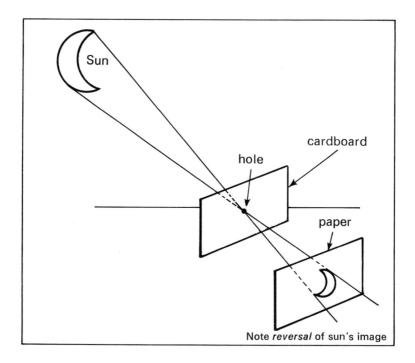

board, you can hold the cardboard as shown in the diagram so that light from the sun goes through the pinhole and falls on a sheet of paper to produce a good image of the crescent-shaped sun.

There are other excellent and safe ways to view a solar eclipse. One is to turn a telescope or pair of binoculars so that the large end is toward the sun. Sunlight goes backward through the instrument to produce a sharp image of the sun's disk on a sheet of paper.

The use of dark glass or a dark film negative is not wise because unless the glass or film is almost opaque, harmful solar rays can still get through to your eyes. And at *no* time should you ever look at the sun through either end of a telescope or pair of binoculars.

13. The moon's surface is covered with mountains that make its rim extremely irregular. It is sunlight streaming through valleys on the moon's jagged rim that produces Baily's beads of light.

Chapter 3: THE MOON

14. Although we speak of the moon going around the earth, it is more accurate to say that the earth and moon form a "two-body system" that revolves around a common center. Because the earth is so much more massive than the moon, this central point is inside the earth. As the earth and moon swing around the center of their system, centrifugal force causes the oceans to bulge upward on the side of the earth directly opposite the moon, producing a second high tide.

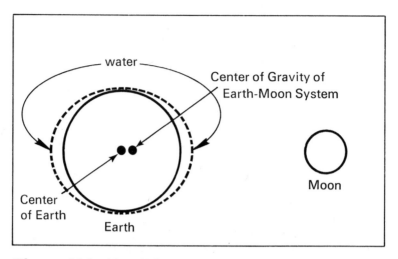

water

Center of Gravity of
Earth-Moon System

Moon

Center
of Earth

Earth

The two high tides. (Distance of the center of gravity of the earth-moon system from the center of the earth is exaggerated to make picture clearer.)

15. The mistakes in the story about the astronauts are:

(1) Stars seen by someone on the moon do not twinkle. Twinkling of stars is caused by movements in the earth's air. Since the moon has no atmosphere, its stars always shine with a steady light.

(2) The moon has no clouds.

(3) The moon has no air to produce a breeze.

(4) Sounds cannot be heard on the moon because there is no atmosphere to transmit sound waves.

(5) Stars can no more be seen inside a crescent earth than we on earth can see them inside a crescent moon. To be visible such stars would have to be *between* the earth and moon. The reason, of course, is that what seems to be empty space inside a crescent earth or moon is not empty at all. It is that part of the sphere that cannot be seen because no sunlight is shining on it.

16. You might be inclined to say that, because the same side always faces us, the moon does not rotate at all on its own axis. To an observer on earth this is true in a sense. Astronomers prefer, however, to view the situation from a spot outside the earth-moon system. Relative to the stars, for example, the moon rotates exactly once on its axis for every revolution around the earth.

An easy way to see this is to put a penny on the table to represent the earth, then move another penny (representing the moon) around the fixed penny, always keeping the same side of the "moon penny" facing the "earth penny." You will find that you have to keep turning the moving penny, and that when it has returned to its starting spot you will have rotated it exactly once.

17. When the moon is very new to us, the earth is very full when seen from the moon. This means that almost the largest possible amount of sunlight is being reflected from the earth to the moon. It is this reflected earthshine that enables us to see faintly the darkened part of the moon when the moon's brightly illuminated portion is only a narrow crescent.

18. No. The reason is that during a high jump an athlete lifts his feet as far upward as possible. This enables him to clear a six-foot bar, even though he has raised his center of gravity much less than six feet.

To make this clear, let's assume the man is six feet tall, as in the following diagram. His center of gravity (the point where all his weight may be regarded as

79

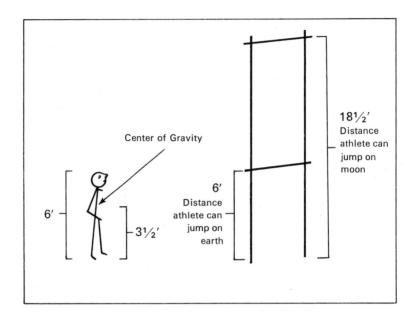

concentrated) is about 3½ feet above ground. When he clears a six-foot-high bar, therefore, he has raised his center of gravity only 2½ feet. On the moon he can raise his center of gravity six times as high, or 15 feet. By jumping as high as he can on the moon, tucking up his legs in the same way he did on earth, the athlete should be able to clear a bar 18½ feet high. This is just over half of the 36-foot jump that is sometimes mentioned in stories about what life would be like on the moon.

Chapter 4: THE PLANETS

19. The nine letters are the initials of the nine planets

in their order from the sun: M̲ercury, V̲enus, E̲arth, M̲ars, J̲upiter, S̲aturn, U̲ranus, N̲eptune, P̲luto.

20. The three words are "rams" (Mars), "heart" (earth), and "arms" (Mars again).

21. Uranus and Saturn. You can change Saturn's "T" to "U," or one of Uranus' "U's" to "T," and the letters will spell the name of the other planet.

22. The ladies *could* indeed have been from Mars and Venus. There is a Mars in Pennsylvania, and a Venus in Pennsylvania, Florida, Nebraska and Texas.

23. No, Mercury has no Twilight Zone. In 1965 astronomers discovered that Mercury does *not* rotate once during each revolution, as the moon does in circling the earth. It rotates *three* times for every two orbits it makes around the sun.

24. Venus is the only planet in the solar system that spins backward. All the other planets, viewed from above their north poles, spin counterclockwise except (as we shall see later) Uranus which has an axis so nearly parallel to the plane on which the planets revolve that its direction of spin is ambiguous. Venus goes clockwise. It spins so slowly that to an observer on Venus the sun would appear to rise slowly in the west and the day would last longer than the planet's year (about 225 earth days).

There is something even stranger about Venus' rotation. Its spin is such that whenever Venus is closest to the earth it always has the same side toward us! No one yet knows why. Astronomers guess that Venus has a lopsided mass that permits the earth to "capture" its rotation in what is called a "resonance lock."

25. Martian "canals," in the sense in which the word is commonly understood, simply do not exist. Many excellent astronomers of the past—notably the Italian Giovanni Schiaparelli and the American Percival Lowell —imagined they saw the planet criss-crossed with hundreds of fine straight lines. They even drew detailed maps of them. Lowell wrote several books in which he

Schiaparelli's map of Martian canals, based on his observations from 1877 to 1886.

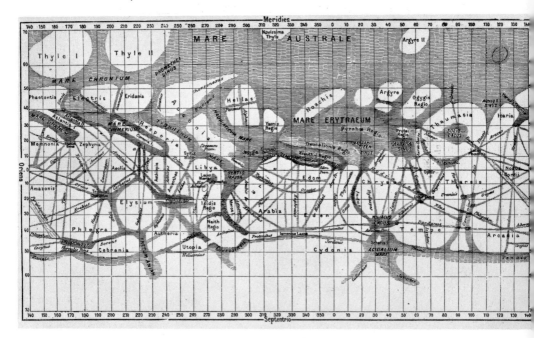

Full view of Mars (left) and closeup of Mars's surface (right), both taken from Mariner spacecrafts, show no indication of the fabled "canals."

argued that the canals must be irrigation ditches dug by Martians to bring water from the polar regions to arid desert areas.

Alas, photographs taken by our Mariner space probes of Mars show no traces of such canals. The surface of Mars is covered with craters, similar to those on the moon. There are also vast craterless regions of wild, disheveled appearance, the nature of which is not yet known.

Most astronomers, in Lowell's time as well as today, were never really able to see Martian canals. The consensus is that the "canals" were partly optical illusions caused by the mind's tendency to group dark spots into lines, and partly a delusion induced by a strong desire to see canals. In telescopes Mars is a tiny, jiggling disk, and only for fleeting moments can one catch a good glimpse of it. In such moments, the mind can play strange tricks with what one thinks he sees. The "canals" of Lowell and other astronomers have never appeared on our photographs of Mars.

One of the most puzzling features of Martian geology has to do with Nix Olympica, a giant crater 300 miles across, much larger than any crater on the moon. Almost at its center is a bright spot, perhaps a peak of some sort, that changes in brightness from year to year. No one yet has offered a convincing explanation of this bizarre phenomenon.

26. The Great Red Spot is a gigantic rosy-colored oval south of Jupiter's equator. It varies in size and

Jupiter's Great Red Spot in two different positions.

shape but is usually about 30,000 miles long and 7,000 miles wide, roughly the area of the earth's surface. The spot drifts slowly east or west to different positions, but it never moves north or south.

The earliest report of someone having seen the Red Spot was in 1664; at that time it was much dimmer than it is today. In 1878 it suddenly became brighter, and it remained bright until 1882 when it began to fade. It had become almost invisible by 1890, after which time it started to brighten again. Since then it has gone through many unpredictable changes in brightness, color, shape, size and position.

What in Jove's name is it? There are two main theories:

(1) *The raft theory*. It is some sort of peculiar solid matter—perhaps a form of frozen water—floating on Jupiter's thick atmosphere like a raft.

(2) *The permanent structure theory*. It is a weird atmospheric condition produced by a fixed bump or hollow on Jupiter's surface. If this is correct, the Red Spot's erratic movements east and west would be the result of changes in the rotation of the planet rather than a movement of the Spot itself.

The truth is that no astronomer knows what the Great Spot is. It is one of the most fascinating mysteries of the entire solar system. Until our space probes begin flying close to the giant planet, astronomers will be able to do little more than make wild guesses.

27. Like our earth, Saturn's axis of rotation is tilted at an angle to the plane of the solar system. For this reason, as the planet goes around the sun we see its rings at different inclinations. About once every 14 years their position is such that we see the rings edge-on. Although the rings are many thousands of miles wide, they are so thin that astronomers estimate their thickness as no more than seven miles; some believe them to be as thin as six inches! Even seven miles is so thin

Saturn's rings are seen at different inclinations as the planet revolves around the sun. When viewed edge-on, as in the pictures at the lower left and upper right, the rings are not visible through a telescope and seem to vanish completely.

that the rings would not be visible in our telescopes at the times when their edges are toward us.

The two blobs of light that Galileo saw in 1610 actually *did* disappear from view. Even today's powerful telescopes would not have been able to see them in 1612 when their disappearance was such a mystifying disappointment to Galileo. The last time Saturn's rings vanished was in 1966. In 1973 they will again reach a period of maximum visibility when the planet tips so that the southern or underside of its rings will be seen.

28. Yes. Many astronomers have argued that Pluto was once a moon of Neptune. The theory is based on Pluto's very slow rotation speed. This is characteristic of moons. If Pluto was indeed a moon that escaped from Neptune to become a planet, it would keep its slow rotation speed.

The escaped-moon theory is also supported by the fact that Pluto's orbit is such an elongated ellipse that at times Pluto is actually closer to the sun than Neptune is. The orbits of the two planets do not now intersect, but they may have done so in the past. Some astronomers have argued that the gravitational influence of Uranus could have caused Pluto to break away from an orbit around Neptune, and in doing so, Pluto may have caused Triton, the larger of Neptune's present moons, to reverse its direction of revolution.

Chapter 5: COMETS AND ASTEROIDS

29. There is no way to tell from the picture which way the comet is moving. A comet's tail always points *away* from the sun because of a solar wind of atomic

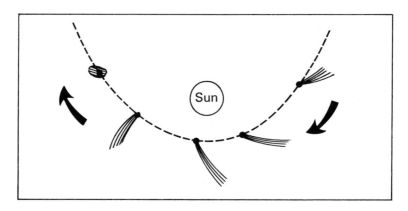

The tail of a comet always points away from the sun.

particles that blows outward from the sun's surface. When a comet approaches the sun its tail streams behind it. At its nearest approach to the sun, the tail is at right angles to the comet's path. As it moves away from the sun its tail streams *ahead* of it! It is impossible, therefore, to tell from a picture of a comet which way it is moving.

30. It is extremely unlikely that the earth will collide with an asteroid, but it is entirely possible. More than a dozen asteroids have paths that cross the earth's orbit. Some cross the orbits of Venus and Jupiter. One asteroid, Icarus (discovered in 1949), actually crosses the orbit of Mercury and goes closer to the sun than any other body in the solar system except for some comets. In June 1968 Icarus missed the earth by about four million miles. This may seem a large distance, but it is only about seventeen times as far as the distance from the earth to the moon. Earlier that year a number

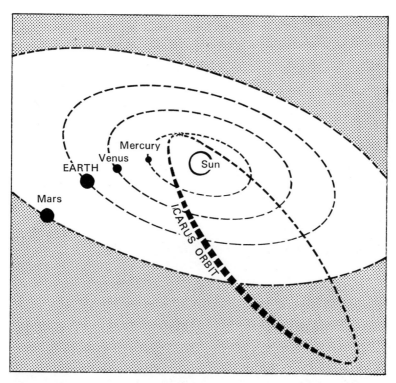

The orbits of the asteroid Icarus and the earth intersect at two points, making collision a possibility.

of ignorant religious cultists had predicted that Icarus would hit the earth and destroy most of its inhabitants. The asteroid's next close approach to the earth will be in 1987. The actual path of Icarus is impossible to plot accurately in advance because it is influenced by so many other planets.

Several asteroids have passed much closer to the earth than Icarus did in 1968. Our closest shave was on October 30, 1937, when Hermes missed the earth by a mere half a million miles, about twice the distance between the earth and moon. Hermes hasn't been seen since. No one knows where the little planetoid is.

Because a collision with a large-sized asteroid could destroy a nation as big as, say, France, Isaac Asimov has predicted that in the future we will have space stations with computers designed to keep a careful radar watch on all approaching bodies. If an asteroid is spotted on a collision course with earth, a spaceship could be sent to explode it with an H-bomb. This would produce, Asimov writes, a harmless shower of meteoric pebbles. "Until then," he concludes, "the Rocks of Damocles remain suspended, and eternity for millions of us may, at any time, be an hour away."

On October 30, 1937, the earth and the asteroid Hermes missed colliding by only half a million miles.

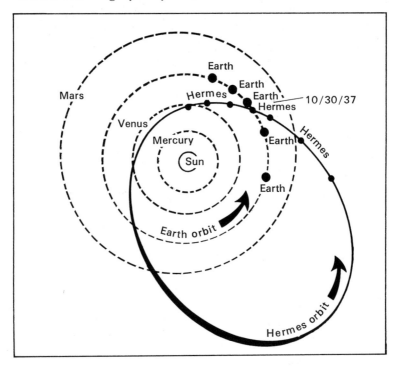

31. "Ekard" is "Drake" spelled backward. The discoverer of Ekard was a student at Drake University in Des Moines, Iowa, when he found the asteroid.

Chapter 6: SPACE FLIGHT

32. Three ways to empty the glass by inertia are:

(1) Hold the glass still, then jerk it quickly in the direction of its base. This will leave the water behind.

(2) Move the glass in the direction of its open end, then suddenly stop it. The water will continue moving forward.

(3) Swing the glass in a circle, open end outward. Centrifugal force (a form of inertia) will propel the water from the glass.

Actually, water would not remain long inside an open glass in zero gravity. With no downward force to keep it in place, adhesion forces would cause the water to creep up the sides of the glass, over its edge and around the outside.

33. The answer to this question is really the same as the answer to the previous one. The spaceship corresponds to the glass, and the water to objects inside the ship. The three ways are:

(1) The ship uses its propulsion system for continuous acceleration (increase in speed) during the first half of its trip. Inertia forces objects toward the back end of the ship, just as your body is forced downward in an elevator when the car accelerates upward. According to Albert Einstein's "Principle of Equivalence," an "inertial field" of this sort is in-

distinguishable from a gravitational field. With the right amount of acceleration, objects inside the ship would behave exactly as if the ship were resting on earth.

(2) The ship uses its propulsion system for continuous deceleration (decrease in speed) during the second half of its trip. This simulates a gravity field as before, except that now the inertial force is toward the *front* of the ship.

(3) The spaceship rotates. Centrifugal force, a form of inertia, causes objects in the ship to move outward from the center of rotation as if a gravitational field surrounded the ship. This is the ideal way to simulate gravity inside a space station that is orbiting the earth. The station could be shaped like an enormous hollow doughnut. By rotating the station at the proper speed, compartments in the station could be given an inertial field of the same strength as gravity on the earth.

These are the only three known ways to simulate gravity in a spaceship. None has yet been used.

34. Not if it remains in one spot. A candle cannot burn unless waste gases from the burning rise upward. This happens on earth because gravity pulls air downward, creating a buoyant force which causes anything lighter than air—the waste gases, for example—to rise. In zero gravity, air has no buoyancy force. Waste gases would stay close to the candle's flame and soon extinguish it. Of course, one could keep the candle burning a long time by moving it slowly from side to side or by blowing gently on it.

35. According to Einstein's theory of relativity the traveling twin will be, after he returns, a trifle younger than his stay-at-home brother. The faster a spaceship moves, the slower time passes inside the ship relative to time on earth. If a spaceship could go as fast as light, time inside the ship would come to a complete stop! (The reasons for this are too complicated to explain, but if you are interested, there is a chapter on the "twin paradox" in my book *Relativity for the Million*.)

If the traveling twin goes a very long distance, at an extremely fast speed, he could age only a few years, then return to earth and find that hundreds of years had gone by! It is theoretically possible, therefore, for an astronaut to travel into the earth's future. (Traveling into the past involves, as science fiction fans know, all sorts of logical contradictions. For example, you could travel back to the time of your childhood, shoot yourself, and therefore prevent yourself from growing up and making the trip backward through time!)

At present the distances and speeds with which astronauts travel are so small that the time difference is not yet measurable. In the future, however, the "twin paradox" may become a reality.

36. Zero gravity would have existed inside Verne's spaceship from the instant it left the cannon's mouth to the time it splashed down in the Pacific. A condition of weightlessness prevails inside any spaceship that is moving freely in space without its rocket propulsion system working.

37. Any object tossed out the window of a moving spaceship would continue to travel away from the ship

because of its inertia. It could not remain alongside the ship as Verne's story has it.

38. The air in a closed half-filled bottle of water would form a sphere in the center of the bottle as shown in the picture. This was actually tested in zero gravity

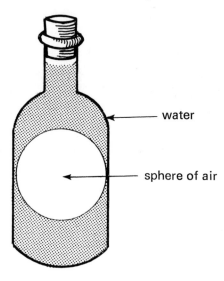

water

sphere of air

by the Russian astronaut, Pavel R. Popovich, during his space flight in 1962. "It [the air] stayed there," he reported, "even when I shook the bottle."

39. The spaceships approach each other with a combined speed of 30,000 miles per hour, or 500 miles per minute. If you imagine the scene going backward in time, like running a motion picture backward, you will see at once that one minute before the ships pass each other they must be 500 miles apart. That distance of 15,537 miles apart at the beginning was added just to confuse you. It is not needed for the simple solution.

40. The rope-yanking technique would not work in a marooned spaceship. It works in a canoe only because there is friction between the canoe and the water. The situation is similar to that of a boy inside a cardboard carton on a polished wooden floor. By moving his body suddenly forward he can make the carton scoot a short distance along the floor. Friction holds the carton in place until the boy's inertia propels the carton forward.

In space there is no friction because the ship is surrounded by an almost perfect vacuum. For this reason, jerking on a rope attached to one end of the ship could not start the ship moving. Every now and then someone who does not understand the basic laws of motion thinks he has invented an "inertial drive" that could propel a spaceship by the force of inertia alone. Such efforts are doomed to failure. The only way a marooned spaceship can start moving is by expelling from it some type of matter, such as the gas from its rocket motors.

41. No, the astronaut would not explode. This is a widespread myth which the motion picture *2001: A Space Odyssey* tried to dispel in a scene which many critics of the film believed to be scientifically wrong. The truth is that some animals have been found able to live as long as several minutes in a vacuum. A human being in outer space could not, of course, survive without air to breathe, but he certainly would not explode. Pressures inside his body are much too weak to cause such an event, even if the astronaut held his breath to keep air inside his lungs. Indeed, he could probably function for 20 seconds or more before he lost consciousness from the effects of cold and lack of air.

INDEX